HULL FC

An Illustrated History

HULL FC

An Illustrated History

Les Hoole

DB
PUBLISHING

First published in Great Britain in 2001 by
The Breedon Books Publishing Company Limited
Breedon House, 3 The Parker Centre, Derby, DE21 4SZ.

This paperback edition published in Great Britain in 2015 by DB Publishing,
an imprint of JMD Media Ltd

ISBN 978-1-78091-465-7

Contents

Acknowledgements

I am indebted to the following people for their loan of images, information and encouragement.

Tim Auty, Mike Green, Dave Makin, Robert Gate, Trevor Delaney, Dianne, Ben and Verity Hoole.

Bibliography
Old Faithful Mike Ulyett and Bill Dalton
Rothmans Rugby League Yearbooks
Rugby League Record Keepers Club booklets

The following newspapers were also consulted:
Hull Daily Mail
Wakefield Express
Yorkshire Post
Manchester Guardian
Halifax Courier

Early Days and The Northern Union

THE Hull Football Club can trace its roots back to 1865 when a group of ex-public schoolboys formed the club, which had its first ground at Woodgates Hall, North Ferriby.

Within five years the club had arranged fixtures with many of the leading West Yorkshire clubs and to ease the travel problems had moved to a ground opposite the Londesborough Arms, Selby. The club prospered and in 1872, by now playing at the Rifle Barracks Field back in Hull, they joined the English Rugby Union. Another ground change saw the club play at Harworth Arms Field, Newland until 1878 when the club moved to a pitch on Anlaby Road.

In 1879-80 season the club merged with junior club Hull White Star, a club which played both association and rugby football at their ground at Hall's Field on Holderness Road. The ground at Holderness was a 12-acre site with a capacity of 5,000 and at the start of the 1885-86 season Hull were granted their first county match.

On 26 October 1894 Hull made the controversial decision to move across the River Hull to take over the Hull Athletic Company's ground at the Boulevard. The ground was used by Kingston Rovers and many thought it unsportsmanlike to take over their junior neighbours' ground. Hull, however could afford the £150 per annum rent, three times what Rovers had paid.

On 21 September 1895 Hull played their first game at the Boulevard and the first home match of the new Northern Union against Liversedge.

The club gradually prospered and by 1908 had fought their way to the Final of the Northern Union Challenge Cup to meet the mighty Hunslet at Fartown, Huddersfield. The London and North Eastern Railway ran seven special trains to Huddersfield and despite atrocious weather conditions a crowd of 18,000 witnessed Hull lose 18-0 to Hunslet.

Hull Football Club season 1895-1896, the very first season at the Hull Athletic Ground, the Boulevard. Following a succession of grounds the nomadic Black and Whites finally settled when they agreed a ten-year lease for £150, three times more than Kingston Rovers could afford.

The following season Hull battled to the Final again this time losing 17-0 to Wakefield Trinity at Headingley.

In 1910 the Airlie Birds defeated Leigh, Batley, Halifax and Salford to once again attempt to lift the Challenge Cup at Fartown. Such was the interest in the game that at kick-off time neither Hull nor their opponents Leeds were at the ground, both stuck in a huge tailback on the rail network between Leeds and Huddersfield. The match eventually kicked off 4.20 but despite holding a 7-2 half time lead the Black and Whites drew 7-7 with the Loiners. The replay was again at Fartown two days later and for the third consecutive time Hull lost 26-12.

In the seasons prior to and after World War One Hull assembled a fine squad and in 1914 finally won the much coveted Challenge Cup.

In 1918-19 they collected the Yorkshire League title for the first time.

The following season, playing with a squad which was a perfect blend of youth and experience, the Airlie Birds were crowned Champions following the 3-2 victory over Huddersfield in the Final.

Cyril Lempriere was one of the clubs early stars, a wingman who had played for Worcester College, Oxford. He captained the side during the last full season at Holderness Road and then at the Boulevard in 1895.

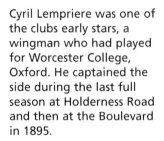

The 1901-02 season saw Hull join the breakaway by the 14 most powerful clubs to form the Northern Rugby Football League, the Edwardian equivalent of today's Super League. Hull finished eighth in the table winning 11 of their 26 games.

Hull depicted on a collectors' card produced by J. Baines of Bradford.

The 'A' team were the winners of the Yorkshire County Junior Challenge Cup in season 1903-04. Back (left to right): Directors Harry Dannatt, L. Whitehead. Standing: H. Fellows, Alf Charlesworth (secretary), F. Sedgwick, C. Sherwood, L.Evans, A. Harrison, J. 'Taffy' Major, A. Higham. Sitting: W. Cook (trainer), G. Lewis, G. Milner, Wilson Harmer (captain), F. Oliver, C. Darcy, J. Ritson. On ground: C. Frank, J. Moxon, George Rogers and Tommy Salt.

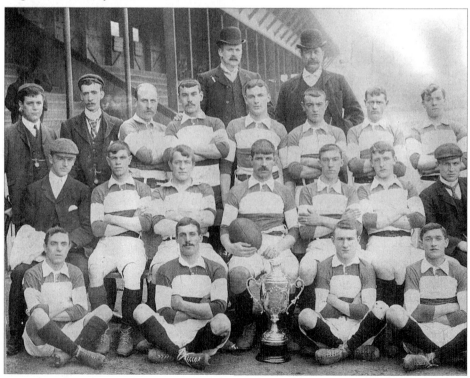

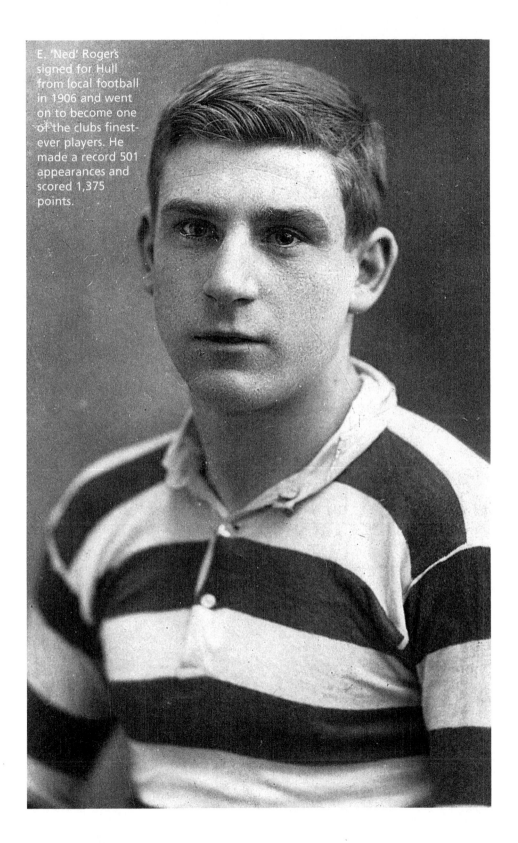

E. 'Ned' Rogers signed for Hull from local football in 1906 and went on to become one of the clubs finest-ever players. He made a record 501 appearances and scored 1,375 points.

George Cottrell made his debut on 5 September 1907 and played 204 games for the Airlie Birds. A powerful centre or wing man he played in all three of Hull's Challenge Cup Final defeats scoring a try in the 1910 Final against Leeds.

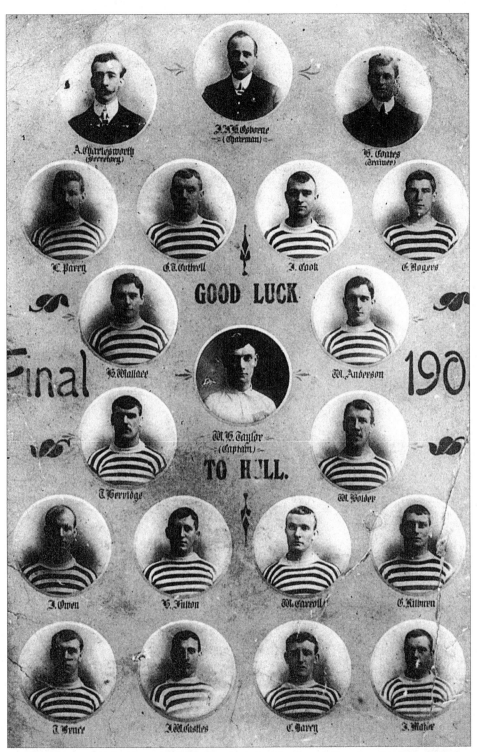

In 1908 the Airlie Birds reached the Final of the Challenge Cup for the first time losing in atrocious weather conditions, which included a second-half snowstorm, to Hunslet at Huddersfield's Fartown.

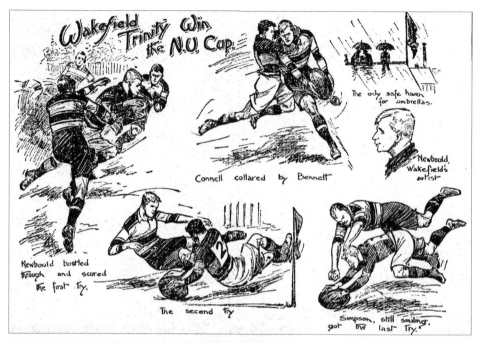

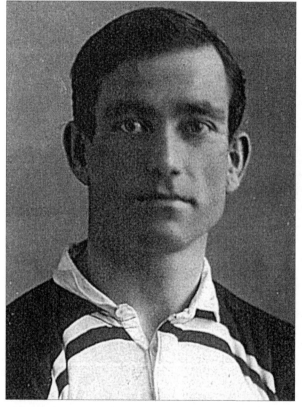

An artist's impression of the 1909 Challenge Cup Final between Hull and Wakefield Trinity at Headingley. Hull had played every round of the cup away from home but once again their form in the Final was abysmal losing 17-0 to Trinity.

Jimmy Devereux was the top try scorer with the first Kangaroos in 1908. He signed for Hull after the tour and went on to make 181 appearances scoring 101 tries.

Dick Taylor
joined Hull in
late September
1909 and made
174 appearances
for the club
scoring 13 tries.

George Cottrell, Tom Herridge, Harry Taylor, Dick Taylor, H. Walton and Ned Rogers relax on the Boulevard pitch.

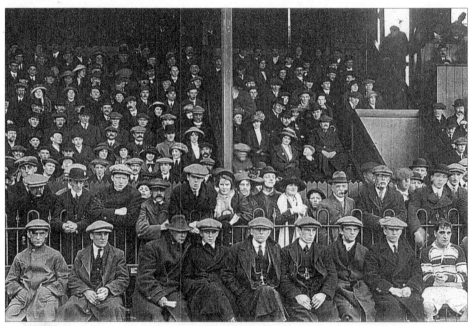

The Hull bench and part of the Boulevard crowd. The player to the right is Billy Anderson.

Ned Holder made just short of 300 appearances for the Airlie Birds and scored 30 tries.

Hooker Tom Herridge, centre George Cottrell, scrum-half Billy Anderson and full-back Ned Rogers stroll to the Boulevard around 1909.

A Baines card featuring Alf Francis.

Frank Boylen signed for Hull from Hartlepool Rugby Union and in 1910 was the Airlie Birds' only representative on the Great Britain Lions tour to Australia and New Zealand. He is second from the left middle row in a Lions team group in Australia.

Hull and Hunslet line up at the Boulevard before the match for the Spring Bank Orphanage Cup.

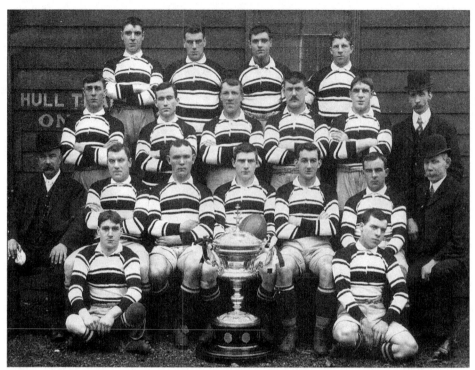

Hull with the Spring Bank Orphanage Cup in 1911-12. Back row (left to right): Arthur Allen, George Connell (captain), Ellis Clarkson and Alf Francis. Third row: Alf Grice, Jimmy Devereux, Billy Holder, Tom Herridge, C. Cappleman and Alf Charlesworth (secretary). Seated: Tom Coates (trainer), George Cottrell, Frank Boylen, 'Ned' Rogers, E. Schofield, A. Barrow, W. Wright (assistant trainer). In front: Gregor Rogers and G. Simpson.

A newspaper cartoon covering the 1913-14 championship competition with Hull and Kingston Rovers looking at the first four of Wigan, Rochdale, Huddersfield and Salford. The Black and Whites finished in fourth place but were beaten 23-5 by Huddersfield in the Championship semi-final.

Alf Grice made 180 appearances for Hull and scored 31 tries in a career that began in September 1911.

Jack Beasty made his debut for the Airlie Birds on Christmas Day 1912 and went to wear the black and white shirt 283 times.

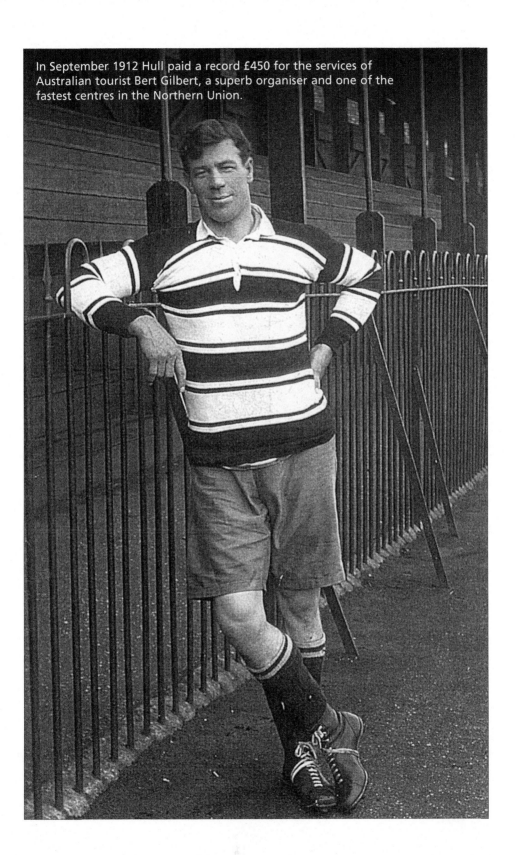

In September 1912 Hull paid a record £450 for the services of Australian tourist Bert Gilbert, a superb organiser and one of the fastest centres in the Northern Union.

Making his debut with Bert Gilbert was fellow Kangaroo Steve Darmody, a strong-running second row forward who played a major part in the Airlie Birds campaigns prior to World War One.

Percy Oldham signed for Hull in 1913 and played just short of 100 games for the Black and Whites.

The Airlie Birds' major rebuilding plans continued in 1913 when Billy Batten was signed from Hunslet for the astounding transfer fee of £600. Batten was reputed to be the highest -paid player in the League and he made 225 appearances scoring 90 tries

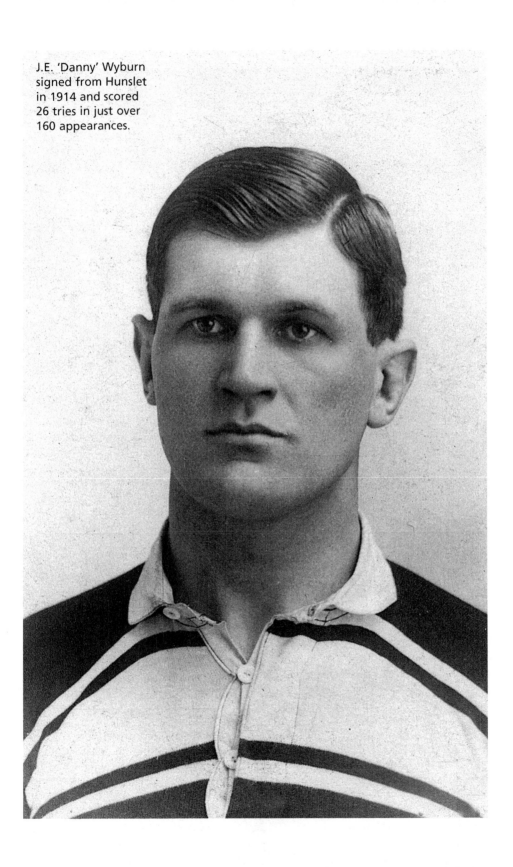

J.E. 'Danny' Wyburn
signed from Hunslet
in 1914 and scored
26 tries in just over
160 appearances.

The Hull bench with, third from left, Ned Rogers, Billy Batten with his young son and Jimmy Devereux.

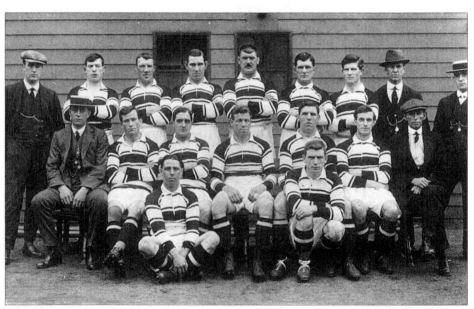

The squad for the 1914-15 season. Standing (left to right): Fred Perrett, Joe Hammill, Billy Holder, Dick Taylor, Tom Herridge, Danny Wyburn, Percy Oldham, Steve Darmody and Greg Rogers. Sitting: Alf Grice, Jimmy Devereux, Billy Anderson, Bert Gilbert (captain), Billy Batten, Jack Harrison and Sid Melville (trainer). In front: Tommy Milner and Ned Rogers.

J.A. Holliday
scored a
solitary try for
the Airlie Birds
in a brief 17-
match career
that began in
April 1914.

Jackie Holdsworth
who made his debut
in April 1914 and
went on to score 69
tries in 158
appearances.

Tommy Milner played 137 games for the Black and Whites and was capped once by Yorkshire.

Alf Francis was the solitary Hull player to tour Australia and New Zealand with the British Lions in 1914. Injuries restricted him to play just three games on the tour but he still managed to score six tries.

Steve Darmody was one of 24 Hull players who joined up during World War One. Darmody tragically lost a foot in an accident while serving with the Motor Transport section in Flanders. In May 1916 a benefit match between West and East Riding teams was played at the Boulevard raising £220 for the Australian.

This is the East Riding team, which won the game 8-6. Standing (left to right): Mr P. Woods (Hull), T.H. Brown (Hull KR), J.E. Kennedy (Hull), J.D. Campbell (Leeds), Tom Herridge (Hull), Steve Darmody, Ned Rogers (Hull), Billy Holder (Hull), L. Fussey (Hull KR), L. Trump (Hull KR), Jack Donaldson (the Australian sprinter) and Mr John Wilson (Hull KR). Kneeling: Tommy Milner (Hull), Alf Francis (Hull), Jimmy Devereux (Hull), Johnny Rogers (Huddersfield) and Frank Boylen (Hull).

The 1918-19 season was split into wartime friendlies and a resumption of Yorkshire League and cup fixtures. The Black and Whites reached the semi-final of the Yorkshire Cup , losing 23-13 to Huddersfield at Fartown. In the Yorkshire League they faired much better collecting the trophy for the first time. Back row (left to right): Mr A.J. Boynton (chairman), Bill Kennedy, Billy Holder, Danny Wyburn, Commander J.W. Kenworthy (MP), Harold Garrett, Alf Grice, Percy Oldham, Tom Herridge and Mr J.R. 'Bob' Pickering (director). Seated: Ted Nolan, Jack Hulme, Arthur Holliday, Billy Batten, Tom Milner, Jimmy Devereaux and Sid Melville (trainer). In front: Jim Kennedy, Alf Francis, Jack Holdsworth and 'Jumbo' Forrester.

Jack Harrison was a local schoolteacher who joined Hull in September 1912. He joined the armed forces and in 1917 after the battle of Oppy Wood he was reported missing in action and was later posthumously awarded the Victoria Cross for valour.

Jim Kennedy was one of Hull's finest goal kickers; he signed in 1915 and kicked 523 goals in 238 appearances.

In late 1919 the Black and Whites signed Eddie Caswell from Cardiff Rugby Union. He collected a Championship medal in his first season of Northern Union football playing in 15 games of the 1919-20 campaign.

The Cup Comes to Hull

THE great disappointment of losing three Challenge Cup Finals in a row led the club to embark on a massive rebuilding campaign which saw many of Hull's finest players come to the Boulevard. Australian's Jimmy Devereaux, Andy Morton and Steve Darmody, Welshman Alf Francis and the great English centre Billy Batten were brought to West Hull and the club's fortunes began to change dramatically.

Batten, who had been a member of Hunslet's 'All Four Cups' side of 1908, was one of the most charismatic and influential players of the era and the club paid a record transfer fee of £600 for his services.

By 1913-14 Hull were one of the leading clubs of the Northern Union and during the season were pushing for both Challenge Cup and Championship honours.

In the first round of the Challenge Cup the Airlie Birds defeated Salford 8-5 at the Boulevard and trounced junior side Featherstone Rovers 27-3 in an ill-tempered second round game at Post Office Road.

The Airlie Birds defeated Halifax 13-0 in a tricky third-round fixture at Thrum Hall.

The semi-final draw paired the Black and Whites with Huddersfield and their 'Team of All the Talent' at Headingley, Leeds.

Led by 'The Prince of Centres' Harold Wagstaff, Huddersfield were at the peak of their awesome powers and were favourites to dispose of Hull and hold on to the Challenge Cup they had won the previous season. Seven thousand Hull supporters left the city to witness the Airlie Birds sweep aside the might and skill of the 'Fartowners' and register one of the club's greatest-ever victories.

Across at Rochdale, Wakefield and Broughton Rangers drew their first semi-final encounter but two days later Trinity were 5-0 victors to set up a re-run of the 1909 Challenge Cup Final.

With the Airlie Birds firmly established as favourites, 11,000 supporters left Hull for the Final at Thrum Hall, all thinking that the

A *Hull Daily Mail* cartoon shows Gilbert of Hull and Carmichael of Kingston Rovers waiting the outcome of the first-round draw of the Challenge Cup.

game was a mere formality.

Wakefield were far from easy opponents however, and it was well into the second half before Hull broke the deadlock with a fine try. Anderson and his stand-off Devereux worked the ball from a scrum straight to Bert Gilbert who fed the advancing Billy Batten well. Batten galloped forward before passing to Jack Harrison who cracked the Trinity defence to score a superb try. In the final minute of the game Alf Francis dashed over to the line to score the try that finally brought the cup to Hull.

Bert Gilbert became the first Australian captain to collect the Challenge Cup and in an effort to evade the thousands of supporters, the Hull team left Thrum Hall in a horse-drawn coach and boarded a train home at nearby Hipperholme station. The cloak-and-dagger return to Hull continued when the players left the train at Hessle and entered the city by horse-drawn coach. A huge reception awaited and as one local paper put it 'The Airlie Birds were the pets of the city.'

Billy Batten with his son Billy junior, on horseback, at the Boulevard.

The squad for the 1913-14 season Back row (left to right): G. Stephenson (director), Jack Harrison, George Cotterill, Jack Beasty. Third row: Alf Grice, Percy Oldham, Billy Holder, Tom Herridge, Dick Taylor and C.H. Cappleman. Second row: J. Chester (director) , Billy Anderson, Jimmy Devereux, Bert Gilbert (captain), Billy Batten, Ned Rogers and Sid Melville (trainer). In front: Alf Francis and Greg Rogers.

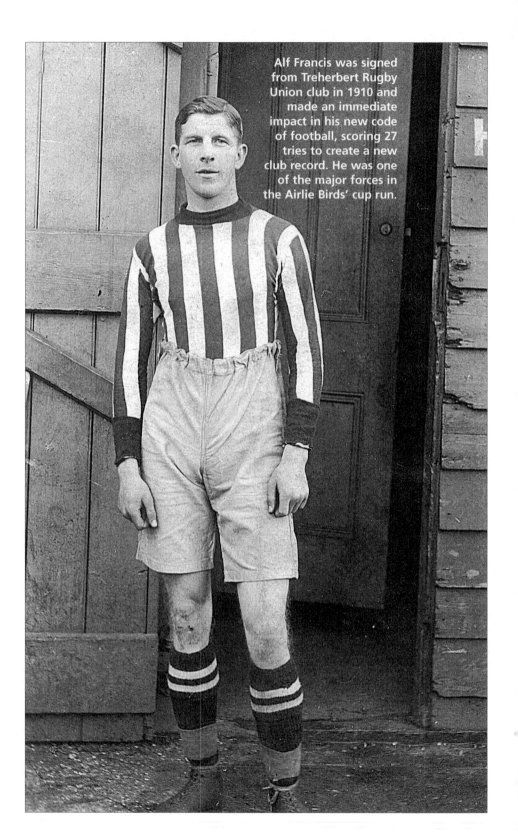

Alf Francis was signed from Treherbert Rugby Union club in 1910 and made an immediate impact in his new code of football, scoring 27 tries to create a new club record. He was one of the major forces in the Airlie Birds' cup run.

Tom Herridge signed for the Black and Whites in 1907 and the big prop was a veteran of Hull's three previous Challenge Cup Finals in 1908-09 and the drawn final and replay defeat in 1910.

Joe Hammill had tasted Challenge Cup success with Dewsbury in 1912 before moving across to Hull in October 1913.

A newspaper cartoon celebrates Hull's first-round victory over Salford at the Boulevard.

Jack Harrison
scored 52 tries
during the 1913-14
season to create a
new club record
that still stands
unbeaten today.

Australian Steve Darmody signs his autograph for a fan at the Boulevard.

TEAMS AND SCORING SHEET FOR TO-DAY.

No.	HUDDERSFIELD.	Goals	Tries	No.	HULL.	Goals	Tries
	FULL BACK.				FULL BACK.		
1	Holland			1	E. Rogers		
	THREE-QUARTER BACKS.				THREE-QUARTER BACKS.		
2	Rosenfeld			2	A. Francis		
17	Gleeson			3	H. Gilbert		
4	Wagstaff			4	W. Batten		
16	Moorhouse			5	J. Harrison		
	HALF-BACKS.				HALF-BACKS.		
18	Rogers			6	J. Devereux		
6	Davies			7	W. Anderson		
	FORWARDS.				FORWARDS.		
15	Chilcott			8	T. Herridge		
10	Clark			9	W. Holder		
11	Gronow			10	J. Hammill		
8	Higson			11	S. J. Darmody		
9	Lee			12	J. P. Oldham		
12	Longstaff			13	R. Taylor		
	RESERVES.				RESERVES.		
7	Jones			14	G. Rogers		
5	Todd			15	A. Allen		
14	Swinden						

Referee, Mr. R. Jones, Widnes. Touch Judges: H. Speight, Wakefield ; T. F. Wilkinson, Hunslet.

The Airlie Birds were drawn against the mighty Huddersfield, the 'Team of All the Talent' and the most successful team in the Northern Union. The line-up for the from the official match programme show some of the finest and most famous names in the game.

Greg Rogers, the brother of Ned, was the reserve for the semi-final at Headingley. He made his debut for Hull in April 1903 and played 130 games for the Airlie Birds.

The semi-final defeat of Huddersfield was one of Hull's finest-ever victories. An artist's impression of the game shows the huge crowds from Hull celebrating the victory by chairing the players shoulder-high from the field.

A newspaper cartoon depicts the 'David and Goliath' victory over Huddersfield in the semi-final.

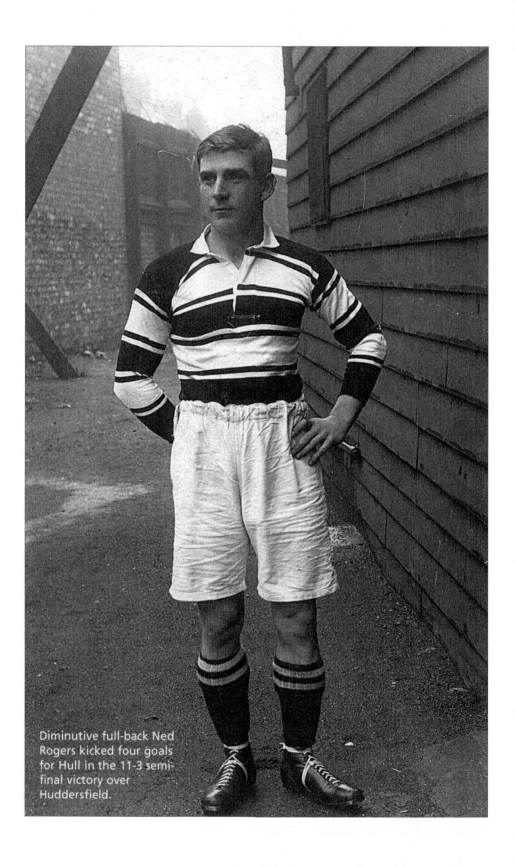

Diminutive full-back Ned Rogers kicked four goals for Hull in the 11-3 semi-final victory over Huddersfield.

Challenge Cup fever swept through West Hull in the days leading up the Final at Thrum Hall, Halifax and prompted P.R. Davies, the local tailoring specialist, to offer the Hull team a pair of trousers each if they brought the cup home.

Mr A.J. Boynton
the Hull FC
chairman for the
1913-14 season.

Billy Anderson the scrum-half for the Challenge Cup Final against Wakefield Trinity had signed for Hull in 1907.

An artist's impression of Hull's first-ever Challenge Cup Final victory.

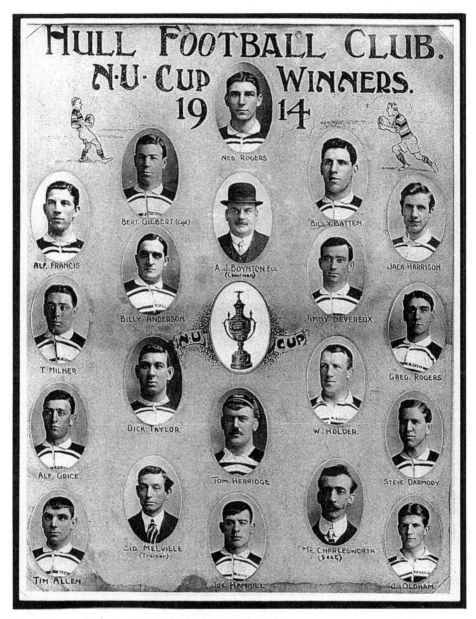

The full squad for the 1914 Challenge Cup campaign.

Alf Grice with the cup at the Boulevard.

A group of players at the Paragon station. Left to right are Devereaux, Gilbert, Darmody, Wyburn, Herridge and Alf Francis with hat in hand.

Hull players and officials ready to board a horse-drawn carriage to parade the cup around the city.

Bert Gilbert the first Australian captain to collect the Challenge Cup holds on tight to the trophy as the team set off. Billy Batten is to the extreme right of the photograph.

Players, officials and well-wishers celebrate the victory at a special dinner.

Billy Batten stands with the Challenge Cup at the Boulevard.

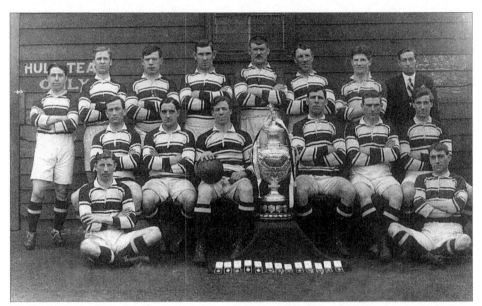

The Hull team with the Challenge Cup at the Boulevard in 1914. Back row (left to right): Milner, Darmody, Hammill, Dick Taylor, Herridge, Holder, Oldham, Melville (trainer). Middle row: Devereux, Anderson, Gilbert, Batten, Ned Rogers, Harrison. In front: Francis and Greg Rogers.

The Twenties

THE Airlie Birds began the new decade in style with a 16-14 Championship Final victory over their rivals across the River Hull, Kingston Rovers. The club was one of the strongest in the League and an average gate of 12,692 watched their progress at the Boulevard. Billy Stone scored 40 tries in the 1920-21 season and toured Australia and New Zealand with the 1920 Lions; Billy Batten captained Yorkshire and received the incredible amount of £1,049 for his benefit match against York. Hull-born Jim Kennedy created two new club records during the season with 14 goals in the 79-2 destruction of Rochdale Hornets and 264 points by the end of the season.

Hull's successful period saw four players selected to oppose the 1921 Kangaroos at Test match level: Billy Batten, Bob Taylor, Billy Stone and Welshman Edgar Morgan, only 36 days after joining the Airlie Birds from Rugby Union.

Consecutive Challenge Cup Final defeats by Rochdale Hornets in 1922 and Leeds in 1923 halted the club's success temporarily but in 1922-23 the Airlie Birds collected the Yorkshire League Trophy.

A trio of Hull men toured Australia and New Zealand in 1924, Bowman and Whitty as players and Mr J.H. Dannatt as tour manager.

In 1923-24 season the Airlie Birds defeated Huddersfield 10-4 at Headingley to capture the Yorkshire Cup for the first time. On their way to the Final the Black and Whites had defeated Bramley, Hunslet and Dewsbury.

In 1924 the great Billy Batten was transferred to Wakefield Trinity for £350 and the following year the popular wingman Billy Stone retired through injury. Batten had played 225 games, scored 90 tries and a solitary goal and Stone, who received £437 from his benefit match, had amassed 527 points from 40 goals and 149 tries in his 222 games for the club.

The Black and Whites ended the 1926-27 season in fifth place and were winners of the Yorkshire League trophy for the third time.

In 1926 the Airlie Birds entertained the New Zealanders at the Boulevard and were unlucky to lose 15-13 in a thrilling game. Harold Bowman and Bob Taylor opposed the Kiwis at Test level for Great Britain during the tour.

The Black and Whites reached the Final of the Yorkshire Cup in 1927 but were no match for a strong Dewsbury side at Headingley.

Joe Oliver joined the club from Batley in 1928 and Bob Taylor was transferred to Barrow, the club he had signed from in 1920.

Harold Bowman and Emlyn Gwynne toured with the 1928 British Lions with Bowman making 14 appearances and scoring 2 tries and Gwynne scoring seven tries in 14 outings.

By the late 1920s the success of the early part of the decade was beginning to elude the Airlie Birds and a series of disappointing league positions and early exits from the knockout competitions prompted the club's directors to embark upon a rebuilding campaign.

Hull finished runners up to Huddersfield in the 1919-20 Championship but a solitary try from Billy Batten in the play-off final against the Fartowners was enough to bring the trophy back to the Boulevard for the first time. Back row (left to right): Beasty, Devereaux, Herridge, Caswell, Newsome, Oldham, Humphries. Third row: Wyburn, Garrett, Taylor, Shield, Grice, Holder, Melville. Seated: Boynton, Holdsworth, Batten, Kennedy, Milner, Markham, Lofthouse. In front: Francis and Hulme.

Harold 'Pete' Garrett made 31 league appearances and scored 11 tries during the championship season.

In January 1920, Hull signed Bob Taylor from Barrow. The highly-mobile forward who became one of Hull's finest played 11 games in the Championship season of 1919-20 and played a total of 308 games for the Airlie Birds.

A caricature of 'Dear old Bob' Taylor.

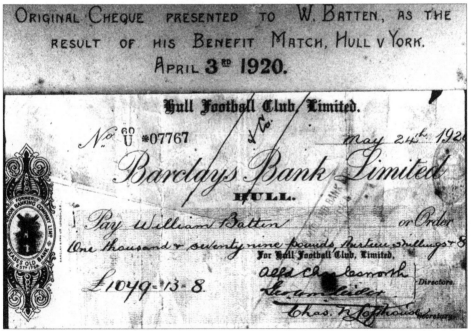

In 1920 Hull granted Billy Batten a benefit game against York, which earned Batten the astounding sum of £1,049 13s 8d.

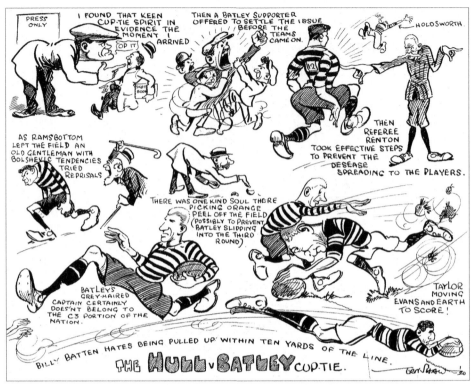

An artist's impression of the Airlie Birds 29-10 victory over Batley in the second round of the 1919-20 Challenge Cup competition.

A caricature of Billy Stone.

Billy Stone a devastatingly fast wingman was signed from Gloucester Rugby Union. A highly popular player with the Boulevard crowds and his team mates Stone went on to score 527 points in 222 games.

Jack Mills, a wing three-quarter, scored six tries in only 16 appearances for the Black and Whites.

Jim Humphries (right), pictured here with Billy Stone on his first team debut in September 1920, made 28 appearances scoring eight tries.

The Airlie Birds were runners-up to Kingston Rovers in the League table but defeated their rivals across the River Hull 16-14 in the play-off Final at Headingley on 7 May 1921. Back row (left to right): Batten (inset), Beasty, Wyburn, Grice, Ellis. Third row: Newsome, Taylor, Charles, Shield, Herridge, Francis, Holdsworth. Seated: Lofthouse, Garrett, Rogers, Kennedy, Devereux, Stone, Humphries, Miller. In front: Milner and Caswell.

A group of players are captured taking a break at Market Weighton en route for the game against York in the 1920-21 season. Standing (left to right): Fred Newsome, Eddie Caswell, Bob Taylor, Alf Grice, Jimmy Devereux, 'Pete' Garrett, Billy Charles, and journalist Mick Goss (Robin Adair). Seated: Alf Francis, Tommy Milner and Ned Rogers. In front: Jim Kennedy and Jack Beasty.

A newspaper artist's impression of a Hull v Hunslet encounter in the early twenties.

Harold Bowman made his debut in December 1921 and went on to make a staggering 451 appearances. He toured Australia and New Zealand with Lions in 1924 and 1928 and made a total of eight appearances for Great Britain and 13 for Yorkshire.

Billy Stone, the Hull captain, checks the coin toss at the 1922 Challenge Cup Final against Rochdale Hornets at Headingley. Despite tries from Batten, Kennedy and Bob Taylor the Black and Whites were defeated 10-9 by the Hornets.

Arthur Moore the Kingston Rovers captain and Billy Stone toss for choice of ends at Craven Street in 1920-21. The game was an eventful one with Moore and Tommy McGiever of Rovers both sent off.

Emlyn Gwynne joined
Hull from Swansea
Rugby Union in 1921
and scored 106 tries in
his Boulevard career

Gwynne toured Australia in 1928 making 11 appearances and scoring 7 tries. He his pictured in his Hull shirt during a training session at the Sydney Cricket ground.

Caricatures of the 1923 Yorkshire Cup winning team.

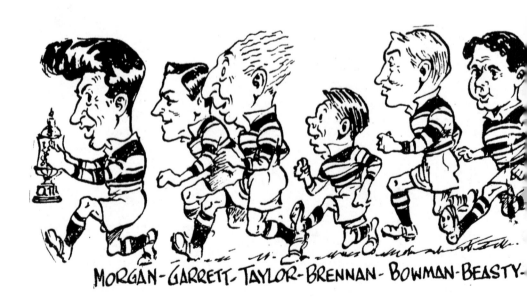

MORGAN - GARRETT - TAYLOR - BRENNAN - BOWMAN - BEASTY

The Airlie Birds finally captured the Yorkshire Challenge Cup on 24 November 1923 defeating Huddersfield 10-4 in the game at Headingley. Standing (left to right): Jack Beasty, Bob Taylor, Harold Garrett, Jim Kennedy, Tom Collins, Claude Ellery, George Oliver, Harold Bowman and Alf Charlesworth (secretary). Seated: Emlyn Gwynne, Eddie Casewell, Edgar Morgan, Billy Batten, Bill Brennan and Ned Rogers. In front: Stan Whitty and Billy Stone.

LL-WHITTY- STONE - BATTEN - KENNEDY-COLLINS AND ROGERS

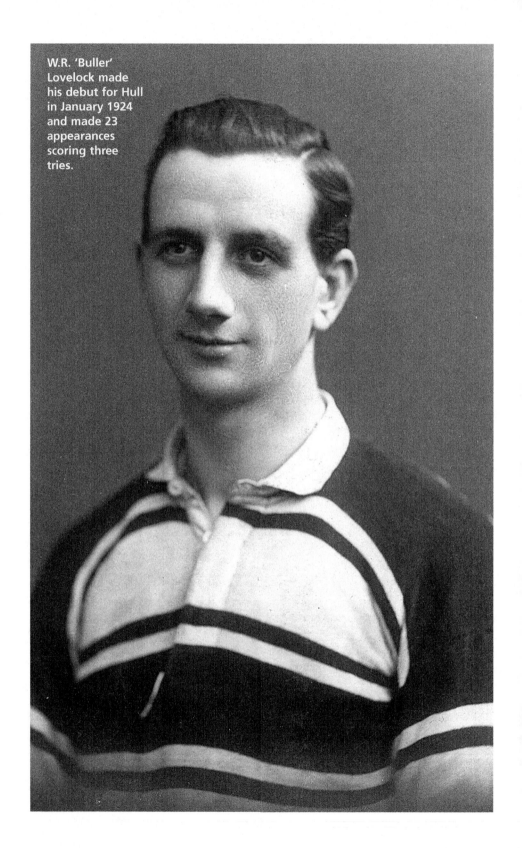

W.R. 'Buller' Lovelock made his debut for Hull in January 1924 and made 23 appearances scoring three tries.

Hull FC are depicted with the other clubs attempting to topple Kingston Rovers from the top of the league table in 1925.

Andrew Carmichael (left) and Joe Oliver were both signed by the Airlie Birds in the late twenties. Carmichael joined Hull from Kingston Rovers and played 244 games for the Black and Whites and Joe Oliver was transferred from Batley, making his Boulevard debut in late October 1928.

Three of the Hull three quarter line up that thrilled the Boulevard crowds during the 1920s: Jack Davies, Tom Collins and Emlyn Gwynne.

Harold Bowman and Australian captain Tom Gorman toss for choice of ends at the Boulevard on 26 October 1929 when a crowd of 10,000 witnessed the Green and Golds defeat Hull 35-2. The other players are (left to right) Lyon and Bob Taylor of Hull and Wally Prigg and Frank McMillan.

The Thirties

THE early seasons of the thirties were a constant struggle for the Black and Whites. In 1931-32 they dropped to 21st place with 21 defeats in 38 games, their worst performance since 1906-07. Gradually things improved, new signings began to make a difference and by 1934-35 Hull had climbed to sixth place in the league table.

Harold Ellerington made his debut on 1 March 1930 and developed into one of Hull's and the games great loose forwards.

In November 1931 Hull dipped into the world transfer market and signed Australian Cec 'Dick' Fifield the international centre from the East's club who had made 22 appearances and scored 8 tries during the 1929-30 Kangaroos tour.

A year later Freddie Miller signed from Crowle Street School. Miller soon developed into one of the clubs greatest full-backs and goal-kickers. He made 385 appearances, including 101 matches in succession and kicked 558 goals.

Around 1934 the Airlie Birds supporters adopted *Old Faithful*, an American cowboy song about a horse, as the club's anthem. The song became popular and is still sung at the Boulevard and wherever the Hull team are playing.

In 1935-36 the years of rebuilding finally paid dividends and the Airlie Birds completed the season in top position and collected the Yorkshire League Trophy for the fourth time. Hull were successful in 23 of their 28 Yorkshire fixtures and were seven points clear of their nearest rivals, Leeds.

The club had used 23 players and won 30 of their 38 games including a double over Kingston Rovers. Top scorer was Joe Oliver who headed both tables with 22 tries and 57 goals for a points total of 180.

In the play-off semi-final Hull beat fourth-placed Wigan 13-2 at the Boulevard and trounced Widnes 21-2 at Huddersfield's Fartown to be crowned Champions for the third time. Joe Oliver crossed for two tries and kicked five goals, Laurie Barlow scored a try and Freddie Miller kicked one goal.

During the season the 28,798 record attendance at the Boulevard was set in the Challenge Cup third-round tie with Leeds. Such was the crush that thousands were forced on to the touchline, only to be showered with cinders by the people on the terraces would could not see.

Harold Ellerington's superb performances during the season caught the selectors' eyes and he toured Australia and New Zealand with the 1936 Lions, making 11 appearances and scoring six tries.

The following season they slumped to seventh position, 11 points behind league leaders, and eventual champions, Salford.

In 1938 the Airlie Birds defeated Bramley, Keighley and Hunslet to oppose Huddersfield in the Yorkshire Cup Final at Odsal Stadium, Bradford.

A brace of goals from full-back Freddie Miller and a solitary try from Corner were not enough to beat a strong Huddersfield side that won the game 18-10.

When World War Two broke out the Black and Whites struggled on playing in the War Emergency Leagues.

Two of the mainstays of the Hull pack during the early 30s were Harold Ellerington (left) and Billy Stead. Hull-born Ellerington joined the Boulevard under-16s in 1925 and made his first team debut in March 1930.

Australian centre Cec 'Dick' Fifield joined Hull in late November 1931. He played 224 games for the Airlie Birds scoring 80 tries and kicking 13 goals.

Joe Oliver, George Bateman and Cec Fifield at the Boulevard in 1934. Bateman was a fine wingman scoring 123 tries in 178 appearances.

Trainer Eddie Caswell and club secretary Everitt Jackson flank Cec Fifield.

Trainer Eddie Caswell tests Ernie Herbert's injured thigh in preparation for the Challenge Cup semi-final with Huddersfield at Headingley in 1935. The player on the left is second row forward Jack Dawson.

Captain Joe Oliver leads the Black and Whites out for the Challenge Cup semi-final at Headingley on 30 March 1935. Harold Ellerington crossed for a try and Oliver kicked a penalty goal but the Fartowners were 21-5 victors.

Ernie Herbert is caricatured on a cigarette card of the 1930s. Herbert played 213 games for Hull scoring 74 tries and kicking six goals.

Four of Hull's finest at the Boulevard: Harold Ellerington, Joe Oliver, Andrew Carmichael and George Barlow.

Hull drew Leeds in the third round of the Challenge Cup in 1936 and a record crowd of 28,798 witnessed the tense encounter at the Boulevard. Harold Ellerington hauls down Leeds wing man Eric Harris.

Airlie Birds' loose forward Harold Ellerington crashes into Leeds full-back Charlie Eaton during the Boulevard cup tie.

Hull Done With the R.L. Cup

No Luck, and Home Record Goes: Leeds Advance: City and Old Hymerians Suffer Defeat

IT was a bad day for Hull teams on Saturday. Leeds won the great cup-tie at the Boulevard. but it was a grim struggle, and there was no luck for Hull.

Leeds entered the semi-final round of the R.L. trophy, the draw for which was due to be made at Leeds to-day.

The result was a keen disappointment for the Hull players and their thousands of supporters. The home record of no defeats since September 22, 1934, went by the board.

Hull lost 5-4 to Leeds in the game and had Joe Oliver and George Barlow sent off. The headline from the *Hull Daily Mail* is short and to the point.

To celebrate the winning of the Championship and the Yorkshire League the players and directors celebrated with a dinner at the Pavilion on 17 June 1936. Back row (left to right): F. Drury (director), Bob Corner, Charlie Booth, Jack Dawson, Fred Miller, George Bateman, Dick Fifield, Eric Overton, Billy Stead, Jim Courtney, Clarrie Gouldstone, Laurie Thacker, Andrew Carmichael, Sid Wilson, Ernie Herbert and Fred Colling. Front row: Eddie Caswell (trainer), Alf Mennell (director), Joe Oliver (captain), George Miller (chairman), Harry Dannatt (president), Fred Foster (director), Phil Woods (director).

Huddersfield and Hull pictured before the game at the Boulevard in 1936. Standing (left to right): Dai Evans, Tom Scourfield, Harry Royal, Langford, Mountain, match referee, Sherwood, Jim Courtney (Hull), Aspinall, Whitehead, Senior, Fiddes (captain Huddersfield), Jack Dawson, The Sheriff of Hull, Freddie Miller, Lord Mayor of Hull, Harold Ellerington, George Miller (chairman), Laurie Thacker, Laurie Barlow, Joe Oliver, Bob Corner, Charlie Booth and Sid Wilson. In front: Madden, Markham, S. Pepperell, Fred Collings, Dick Fifield and George Barlow.

A practice match at the Boulevard in late August 1937. Left to right are Eric Overton, Jack Dawson, Tommy Fletcher (with the ball), Laurie Barlow, George Barlow and Billy Stead.

Frank Hurley, an Australian centre, signed for Hull in 1937 and made his debut on 17 April 1937. He made 67 appearances scoring 29 tries.

A try at the Boulevard against Huddersfield for right wingman Sid Wilson in 1937. The Huddersfield tackler is Langford and the other players are Sherwood, S. Pepperell and Madden.

Action from a Hull v Wigan League encounter at the Boulevard in the mid-thirties. Referee Holbrook watches closely as Wigan centre Gordon Innes kicks while flanked by Hull's Laurie Thacker and Laurie Barlow.

Harold Ellerington the Hull captain shakes hands with Australian captain Wally Prigg prior to the tour game at the Boulevard in 1937. The Kangaroos won the game 22-12 witnessed by a crowd of 15,000.

Huddersfield's Ray Markham evades the grasp of Hull's Australian wingman Frank Hurley with Harold Ellerington closing in to cover the break.

R.J. Hogg made his Hull debut on 11 December 1937 and made 38 appearances scoring four tries.

The cover and line up from the programme issued by Hull for the 1938 Yorkshire Cup Final against Huddersfield at Odsal in 1938. Hull lost 18-10 to the Fartowners with Ellerington and Corner scoring tries and Freddie Miller kicking two goals.

Huddersfield Captain Alex Fiddes and Hull Captain Harold Ellerington shake hands before the 1938 Yorkshire Cup Final, the first to be played at Odsal Stadium, Bradford.

Airlie Birds Ellerington, Booth and Laurie Barlow close in on a loose ball during the 1938 Yorkshire Cup Final.

1938 Challenge Cup Action as Hull's Tommy Johnson looks to pass out wide with Kingston Rovers wingman Jack Spanner blocking his path.

Joe Oliver moved across the river to play for Kingston Rovers in 1937 before returning to the Boulevard in 1943. He scored a club record 687 goals and 1,842 points during his Boulevard career. Hull and Rovers were paired in the first round of the Challenge Cup in February 1938 and the rival captains Ellerington and Oliver shake hands at Craven Park before the match, which Kingston Rovers won 8-5.

Hull's squad for the 1939-40 season. Standing (left to right): G. Barlow, L. Barlow, J. Dawson, E. Wray, C. Booth and Eddie Caswell (trainer) Sitting: W. Morrell, F. Miller, E. Herbert (captain), A. Bowers, W. Docker and Stan Brogden. In front: T. Johnson and F. Hurley.

The Forties and Fifties

HULL continued to play on during World War Two despite the handicap of having 33 players in the armed forces and the East Stand destroyed by an enemy bombing raid in 1941.

Several players were 'on loan' from other clubs including Huddersfield, Swinton and Kingston Rovers. During the conflict Laurie Barlow earned the Military Medal for his actions in the Middle East and the club lost Ernie Herbert who died a few days after his discharge and Jack Dawson who died on duty with the RAF.

The club struggled to make progress in the first season after the war and a total of 46 players were used in the first peace time campaign. By 1946-47 season the Airlie Birds had reached the Yorkshire Cup Final for the seventh time but were defeated by 10-0 by Wakefield Trinity at Headingley.

A massive rebuilding of the team began in the late 1940s and early 1950s with some superb and famous names signing for Hull. Roy Francis joined from Warrington, Tommy Harris and Bill Hopkins came north from Welsh Rugby Union, Mick Scott from Boulevard Juniors, Johnny Whitley from Hull Boys Club, Colin Hutton was transferred from Widnes and Jim Drake signed from York amateur side Heworth.

In 1953 Colin Hutton established a new club scoring record with 303 points from four tries and 144 goals but despite this the club slumped to 15th place in the League table. Three successive Yorkshire Cup Final defeats in the mid-fifties did little to instil confidence in the supporters but by 1955 the Airlie Birds were crowned Champions for the fourth time. The Black and Whites had finished in fourth place and defeated Warrington 17-0 at Wilderspool to oppose Halifax in the Final at Maine Road, Manchester. A dramatic last-minute penalty-kick from Colin Hutton gave Hull a single-point victory and the Championship for the first time since 1936.

The following season Hull finished in second place but, having trounced Barrow 45-14 in the semi, lost 15-14 to Oldham at Odsal Stadium, Bradford.

The 1957-58 season saw Hull finish in fourth place and once again they entered the Final when they defeated Oldham 20-8 at the Watersheddings. A huge Odsal crowd of 57,699 saw the Black and Whites defeat Workington Town 20-3 to collect the Championship trophy.

In 1959 Hull defeated Blackpool Borough, Wakefield Trinity, Hull Kingston Rovers and Featherstone Rovers to reach the Challenge Cup Final for the first time since 1923. Hull made their debut at Wembley against the mighty Wigan and despite five goals from Arthur Keegan and a try from scrum-half Finn the Airlie Birds were outclassed and beaten 30-13.

In the final season of the successful decade Hull played their way to Wembley again with victories over York, Keighley, Wigan and Oldham. An injury-ravaged side battled bravely but the sheer pace of Wakefield Trinity was enough to give them a record 38-5 victory.

RUGBY LEAGUE FOOTBALL

AT THE
BOULEVARD,

SEPTEMBER 1943,
TO
MARCH 1944.

HULL'S LIST
OF
HOME FIXTURES.
1943.

September	4th.	BATLEY.
"	11th.	WAKEFIELD TRINITY.
"	25th.	HUDDERSFIELD.
October	9th.	HALIFAX.
"	16th.	HUDDERSFIELD.
		(1st Round Yorks. Cup)
November	13th.	HUNSLET.
"	27th.	BRADFORD.
December	11th.	KEIGHLEY.
"	27th.	(Boxing Day) YORK.
		1944.
February	5th.	DEWSBURY.
"	19th.	FEATHERSTONE.
March	11th.	1st. Round R. L. CUP.
"	25th.	LEEDS.

PRICES OF ADMISSION.

East (Best) Side - 2/3d.   West Side - 1/6d.
Ladies and H.M. Forces in Army, Navy or R.A.F. Uniform.
East Side - 1/-   West Side - 7d.
(All including Entertainment Tax).

The Boulevard is a Home of Sociability and Sport.
Hull have 39 pre-war Players in H.M. Forces.
The Lads write light-heartedly of their "stiff work out yonder ;" "glad the Club is carrying on, despite difficulties ;" "long to resume at the Boulevard ;" and "hope every Hull Supporter is encouraging all available players keen to keep Hull's Rugby League Flag flying.
One popular Hull first teamer writing from the Middle East gives a "DOUBLE EVENT."
(1) "Hull F.C's, No Surrender and a good number of Match Wins."
(2) "A Glorious Victory for the Allies."
        WHAT MORE NEED YOU ASK ?

A fixture card for Hull's War Emergency League season of 1943-44. The Airlie Birds played 21 games winning 15 and losing six to finish in third place.

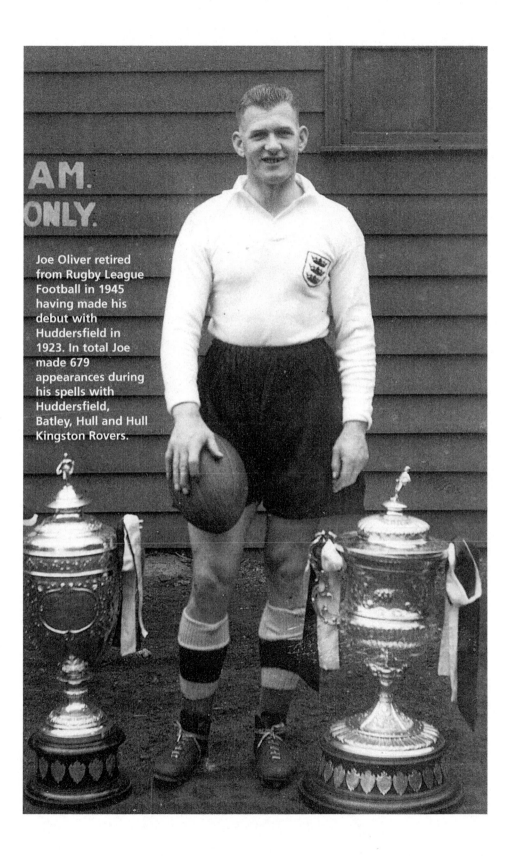

AM.
ONLY.

Joe Oliver retired from Rugby League Football in 1945 having made his debut with Huddersfield in 1923. In total Joe made 679 appearances during his spells with Huddersfield, Batley, Hull and Hull Kingston Rovers.

In 1947 Hull defeated Kingston Rovers 15-11 in the semi-final of the Yorkshire Cup. Action from the Final against Wakefield Trinity at Headingley shows Trinity's Baddeley collecting the ball.

Wakefield defeated Hull 10-0 before a crowd of 29,000 at Headingley. I.J. Watts races to cover a Wakefield break.

Australian left wingman Bruce Ryan made his debut for the Black and Whites against Castleford at the Boulevard on 23 August 1947, his first of 84 games. He is captured crashing through the Castleford defence with Hand and Sullivan in support.

The Hull team for the league match against Batley on 31 January 1948. Back row (left to right): Tattersfield (coach), Booth, Evans, Jewitt, Tindall, Ryan, Sullivan, Kavanagh, Watt and trainer Eddie Caswell. Seated: Miller, E. Bedford, Madden, Lawrence (captain), Jackson, Bowers, Bedford and Sinclair.

Bruce Ryan moves to tackle a Belle Vue Rangers forward during the league game with the long-gone Manchester-based club on 6 September 1947.

Action from the Hull v Australia tour match at the Boulevard on Thursday, 28 September 1948.

Joe Sullivan is tackled by Alec Docker (13), Bryn Goldswain (12) and Benny Schofield during the Good Friday derby match with Kingston Rovers at the Boulevard.

The Kangaroos were given a stern test by the Black and Whites but watched by a crowd of over 16,000 the tourists were 13-3 winners.

The 1950-51 season saw Hull finish in 18th place in the League table, winning 15 and drawing two of their 36 games. Back row (left to right): Hagen Evans, Carl Turner, Des Foreman, Arthur Bedford, Les Baxter, Tom Hart, Tom Danter and Roy Francis. In front: Tom Harris, trialist, Keith Gittoes, Dennis Rushton, Ernie Lawrence and Don Burnell.

Australian centre or wing Keith Gittoes made his debut for Hull on 23 September 1948 and made a total of 123 appearances, scoring 41 tries.

The squad for the Challenge Cup tie at Warrington after the special training session at the Boulevard on Friday, 9 February 1951. Standing Joe Clark, Bill Hopkins, Des Foreman, Arthur Bedford, Les Baxter, Tom Hart and Jack Murray (trainer). Seated: Keith Gittoes, Ivor Watts, Roy Francis, Don Burnell and Tom Harris. In front: Gerry Cox and Duncan Jackson.

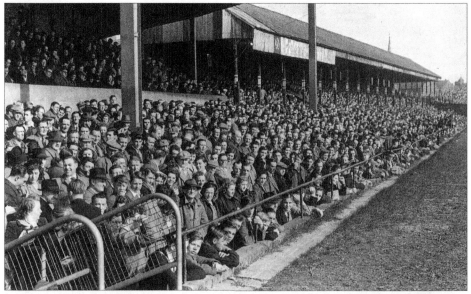

Crowds pack the East Side for the derby game against Kingston Rovers during the fifties.

Johnny Whiteley, one of Hull's finest forwards makes a typical surging run. He made his debut for Hull on 23 December 1950 and went on to play 417 games, scoring 156 tries and kicking two goals.

The Hull team for the league game against Batley at Mount Pleasant in 1951. Back row (left to right): Pat O'Leary, Joe Clark, Tom Hart, Des Foreman, Dennis Rushton, S. Harrison, Tom Danter, and Arthur Bedford. Sitting: Mick Scott, Ernie Lawrence, Roy Francis, Keith Gittoes and Tom Harris. In front: Ivor Watts and Don Burnell.

A Hull team from the 1952-53 season when the Airlie Birds finished in 17th place in the league table. Standing: Mick Scott, John Watkinson, Carl Turner, Des Foreman, John Whiteley, Harry Markham and Robin Coverdale. In front: Ivor Watts, Pat O'Leary, Bernard Conway, Tom Harris, Colin Hutton and Charlie Knapp.

The squad for the Challenge Cup-tie against Widnes assemble early to catch their train. Left to right are O'Leary, J. Murray (trainer), Bowman, Knapp, Coverdale, Markham, Watts, Scott, E. Hardaker (chairman), Bedford, Riches, Harris, Watkinson, Hockley and Hutton.

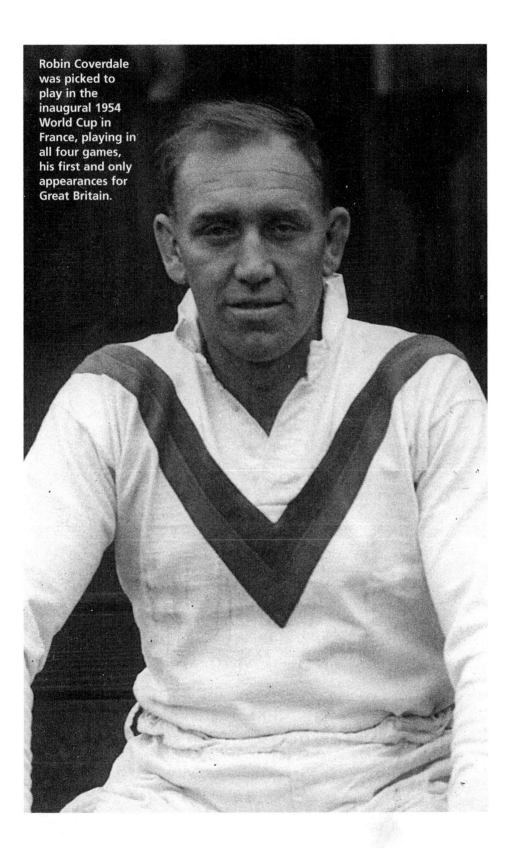

Robin Coverdale was picked to play in the inaugural 1954 World Cup in France, playing in all four games, his first and only appearances for Great Britain.

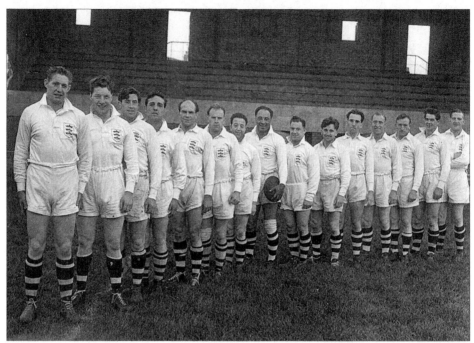

The Hull squad for the final training session before the Yorkshire Cup Final against Halifax at Headingley on 23 October 1954. Left to right are John Whiteley, Mick Scott, Arthur Bedford, Norman Hockley, Colin Hutton, Bernard Conway, Albert Tripp, Roy Francis, Tom Harris, Ivor Watts, Carl Turner, Robin Coverdale, Bill Riches, Bill Drake and Harry Markham. The Black and Whites were defeated 22-14 by Halifax.

The combined Hull and Hull KR 13 pack into the Boothferry Park dressing-room before the game against Australia on 15 October 1956. Over 17,000 people attended the Monday night game, which the Kangaroos won 37-14.

Tommy Harris plants the down for a try during the 1955-56 Championship Final at Manchester City's Maine Road ground. Following the Welsh hooker is a delighted Johnny Whiteley.

With the score at 9-8 to Halifax the Airlie Birds were given a dramatic last-minute penalty which Colin Hutton kicked from the touchline to give Hull a one-point victory and the Championship for the first time since 1936.

The programme cover for the 1956-57 game against Featherstone Rovers.

RUGBY LEAGUE FOOTBALL

★

INTERNATIONAL
CLUB
CHAMPIONSHIP

HULL

English R.L. Champions, 1955/6

VERSUS

ALBI

French R.L. Champions, 1955/6

Souvenir
Programme 3d.

No 1712

In 1957 the English champions and runners-up played their French counterparts for the European Club Championship. Hull won five and drew one of their six games and were crowned European club champions. In April 1957 they entertained French champions Albi at the Boulevard. Here is the cover of the match programme and the teams.

Tommy Harris with the magnificent shield awarded to the winners of the European Club Championship.

Season 1957-58 was one of Hull's finest with 27 victories and 930 points scored. Ivor Watts (far left on front row) was the top try-scorer with 28 touchdowns from 27 games.

The team which defeated Leeds 41-25 in the league game at the Boulevard in August 1957. Back row (left to right): G.W. Sharpley (trainer), Jim Drake, Carl Turner, Colin Cole, Bill Drake, Mick Scott and Peter Bateson. In front: Ivor Watts, Geoff Dannatt, Tommy Finn, John Whiteley, Tom Harris, Bill Coulman and Stan Cowan.

A crowd of 27,000 attended the Good Friday derby match with Kingston Rovers at the Boulevard in 1958. The team which beat Rovers 15-8 are: Back row (left to right): Jim Drake, Brian Hambling, Geoff Dannatt, Bill Drake, Brian Cooper, Mick Scott and Peter Bateson. In front: Brian Saville, Ivor Watts, Johnny Whiteley, Tommy Finn, Tommy Harris and Frank Broadhurst.

The Black and Whites ended the 1957-58 campaign in second place and defeated Oldham 20-8 in the play-off semi-final at the Watersheddings. The line-up for the Championship Final against Workington Town at Odsal Stadium, Bradford, is (back row left to right): Cyril Sykes, Alan Holdstock, Brian Saville, Peter Whiteley, Geoff Dannatt, Peter Bateson and Mick Scott. In front: Brian Cooper, Brian Hambling, Tommy Finn, Johnny Whiteley, Ivor Watts and Frank Broadhurst.

A determined Workington defence cut short a Hull attack during the Championship Final at Odsal. The match was attended by a huge crowd of 57,699.

The dramatic sequence of events as Mick Scott charges for the line, lunges and then plants the ball down firmly for one of Hull's four tries in the 20-3 Championship Final victory over Workington Town.

A Black and Whites team from season 1958-59 when the club finished in seventh position in the League table with 51 points. Back row (left to right): Brian Saville, Cyril Sykes, Bill Drake, Mick Scott, Peter Bateson, Jim Drake. Middle: Stan Cowan, Brian Cooper, John Whiteley (captain), Tommy Harris, Brian Hambling. Front: George Matthews, Ivor Watts, Roy Francis (coach), Dick Bonstead, Tommy Finn.

In 1959 Hull reached their seventh Challenge Cup Final and made their first appearance at the Empire Stadium, Wembley. The Wembley squad are pictured at Paragon station ready to make the journey to London.

THE RUGBY LEAGUE CHALLENGE CUP COMPETITION

FINAL TIE

HULL

v

WIGAN

SATURDAY, MAY 9th, 1959   KICK-OFF 3 pm

EMPIRE STADIUM

WEMBLEY

An attack of the famous 'Wembley nerves' did little to help their play and a superb Wigan side were comfortable 30-13 winners.

In November 1959 Tommy Harris (third from right front row) and Johnny Whiteley (fourth from right back row) were members of the Great Britain side that defeated Australia in the Second Test at Headingley. With the score at 10-6 to the Kangaroos and around a quarter of an hour left to play the two Hull forwards helped to give the British a famous victory. Hooker 'Bomber' Harris heeled the ball cleanly from the scrum; York's Jeff Stevenson flashed a pass to the charging Whiteley who crashed his way over for a try.

The Sixties and Seventies

THE start to the sixties was a disastrous one; the club slumped to 16th place and for the first time for 31 years finished below East Hull rivals Kingston Rovers.

The Rugby Football League went back to a two-division system in 1962-63 and Hull avoided relegation by just three points. The following season the Airlie Birds could only manage four victories from 30 games and were relegated along with Keighley.

The two-division experiment lasted for just two campaigns and the Black and Whites ended the 1964-65 season in a much-improved 13th place with 19 victories from 34 games.

Several famous names left the Boulevard around this period. Jim Drake moved across to Craven Park, Tommy Harris joined York as coach, and coach Roy Francis went to Leeds. Johnny Whiteley was appointed club coach.

On 9 December 1961 two new wingmen made their Boulevard debuts against Bramley, Wilf Rosenberg and Clive Sullivan. South African Rosenberg known as 'The Flying Dentist' crossed for two tries and on the opposite wing Clive Sullivan scored a hat-trick. Rosenberg was to stay at the Boulevard for 87 games and 42 tries while for Sullivan it was the beginning of a marvellous Rugby League career that would embrace both the city's clubs. By the end of his career Sullivan had made 347 appearances for Hull and scored 250 tries and his career totals were 629 games, 406 tries and 1,218 points.

The Yorkshire Cup Final of 1967 ended in deep disappointment when the Airlie Birds lost by a single point to Kingston Rovers at Headingley. Davidson scored a try and a goal and Arthur Keegan kicked one goal but it proved too little to defeat the Robins.

Two years later the Black and Whites were in the Final again this time defeating Featherstone Rovers 12-9 to collect the cup for the second time.

A return to two divisions in 1973-74 saw Hull languish in the lower grouping until 1976-77 when they returned to the top flight as Champions with 22 wins from 26 games. During the season the club appointed former Kingston Rovers player and coach Arthur Bunting as coach and although results improved the Airlie Birds were relegated.

The following season Bunting signed Steve Norton and Sammy Lloyd from Castleford and the club swept all before them to win promotion with 26 victories from 26 games. Lloyd in his first season at Hull smashed two club records with 170 goals and 369 points.

In 1979 the astute Bunting brought a throng of highly-talented players to the Boulevard and the Airlie Birds became one of the major forces in the game.

The sleeping giant of Hull FC had been aroused and in December 1979 a crowd of 18,500 packed the Boulevard to witness the Black and Whites defeat Kingston Rovers 13-3 in the BBC2 Floodlit Trophy Final. It was the prelude to one of the clubs most successful and exciting decades.

Pictured after a training session at the Boulevard in 1959-60 are (back row, left to right): Jim Drake, Tommy Harris, Cyril Sykes, Johnny Whiteley, Bill Drake, Brian Cooper, Mick Scott and Peter Bateson. In front: Tommy Finn, Frank Broadhurst, George Matthews, Brian Saville, and Stan Cowan.

Mick Scott was one of Hull's finest forwards. He made his debut in 1949 and made a total of 459 appearances before his retirement in 1963.

Hooker Tommy Harris and prop Sam Evans are pictured in Hull town centre with their 1960 Wembley blazers. Evans had played most of his career with Kingston Rovers before joining the Airlie Birds for just 17 appearances.

In May 1960 Hull reached the Challenge Cup Final for the second successive season but once again their performance was a great disappointment. Mick Smith, seen here being tackled by Wakefield's Jack Wilkinson made his Hull debut in the Final.

Wakefield's South African centre Alan Skene is tackled by David Johnson with Halafihi in support.

THE RUGBY LEAGUE CHALLENGE CUP COMPETITION

FINAL TIE
HULL
v
WAKEFIELD TRINITY

SATURDAY, MAY 14th, 1960   KICK-OFF 3 p.m.

EMPIRE STADIUM

WEMBLEY

OFFICIAL PROGRAMME   ·   ONE SHILLING

The programme cover for the Final which Wakefield Trinity won 38-5. Tommy Harris who left the field for part of the game with concussion was awarded the Lance Todd Trophy for his superb display.

Johnny Whiteley is stopped in his tracks by two Wakefield tacklers. Despite losing, Hull gained some consolation from a stunning first-half performance during which they matched Wakefield well.

The Hull squad for the 1960-61 season. Back row (left to right): David Doyle-Davidson, Gordon Harrison, Cyril Sykes, Bill Drake, Brian Hambling, Mick Scott and Jim Drake. Seated: Terry Hollindrake, Jack Kershaw, Tommy Harris, Johnny Whiteley, Stan Cowan, Frank Broadhurst and Ralph Walters. In front: George Matthews and Tommy Finn.

Johnny Whiteley is in the thick of the action in an explosive incident during the Great Britain v France World Cup match at Swinton in 1960.

Hull's 13 for the league game against Hunslet at Parkside in early February 1962 which the Black and Whites won 10-0 thanks to a try from Kershaw and a try and two goals from Bill Drake. Back row (left to right): Terry Hollindrake, Brian Hambling, Ian Corban, Clive Sullivan, Bill Drake, Jack Kershaw, Charlie Booth and Trevor Whitehead. Kneeling: Arthur Keegan, Stan Cowan, Johnny Whiteley, Tommy Finn and George Matthews. Welshman Sullivan made 347 appearances for the Black and Whites scoring 250 tries. He was capped 17 times by Great Britain and played for Wales five times.

Welshman Sullivan made 347 appearances for the Black and Whites scoring 250 tries. He was capped 17 times by Great Britain and played for Wales five times.

Clive Sullivan was one of the city of Hull's finest players. A naturally talented wingman he scored a hat-trick of tries on his debut for the Airlie Birds on 9 December 1961.

Season 1961-62 was a poor one for the Black and Whites they finished in 16th position with 18 victories from 36 games. Back row (left to right): Jim Drake, Peter Bateson, Terry Hollindrake, Bill Drake, Malcolm Storey, Brian Hambling, Brian Saville and George Matthews. In front: Tommy Harris, Tommy Finn, Mick Scott, Stan Cowan and Frank Broadhurst.

A combined Hull-Hull KR 13 met the touring Kangaroos on 12 December 1963 at Boothferry Park. The Australians ran out 23-10 victors watched by a crowd of 10,481.

Johnny Whiteley was originally a military policeman before joining brewers Moors and Robson's as a delivery driver. He retired as player from Hull in 1965 to concentrate more on coaching.

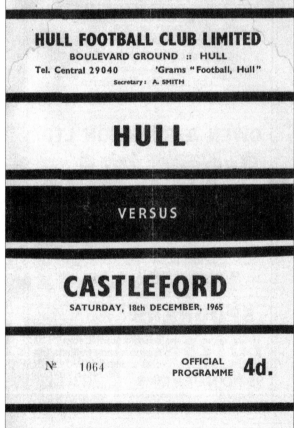

HULL FOOTBALL CLUB LIMITED

BOULEVARD GROUND :: HULL

Tel. Central 29040   'Grams "Football, Hull"

Secretary: A. SMITH

HULL

VERSUS

CASTLEFORD

SATURDAY, 18th DECEMBER, 1965

№ 1064   OFFICIAL PROGRAMME **4d.**

A programme cover from the 1965-66 season.

A flashpoint in a league match at Parkside during the sixties when Hull's Jim Neill and Hunslet's Kenny Eyre are both sent from the field for fighting.

The referee is still at it, and eventually they go.

Hull had three players selected for the Great Britain v France game at Carcassonne in January 1967. Mick Harrison, Arthur Keegan and Clive Sullivan are pictured at the Boulevard celebrating their call up with Hepworth and Hardisty of Castleford. Sullivan and Hepworth scored two tries each as the British beat France 16-13.

The Airlie Birds' great connection with the city's fishing industry is demonstrated as the Hull team line up for a minutes silence to remember the loss of the trawlers *St Romanus* and *Kingston Peridot* before the game with Wigan on 3 February 1968.

The Hull side for the league game with Hunslet at the Boulevard on 6 September 1969. Back row (left to right): Johnny Whiteley (coach), David Jervis, Chris Forster, Howard Firth, Alan McGlone, Nick Trotter, Mike Harrison, Jim Macklin, Joe Brown and Brian Hancock. In front: David Doyle-Davidson, Ken Huxley, John Maloney, Arthur Keegan, Chris Davidson and Clive Sullivan.

Keith Boxall made three appearances for Yorkshire, scoring two tries. Here he is presented with his Yorkshire cap for the 1971-72 season.

At the end of the 1971-72 season Hull finished in 19th place with 16 victories in 34 games. Standing (left to right): Jim Harrison, Tony Dukes, Nick Trotter, Harry Aston, Mike Crane, Alf Macklin and Howard Firth. In front: Keith Boxall, Mike Kendle, Brian Hancock, Terry Kirchin, Ken Foulkes and Terry Devonshire. Mascot Kevin Hall.

The vastly experienced Steve 'Knocker' Norton was signed from Castleford for £25,000 and the international made his debut on 29 January 1978. Norton, pictured here scoring a try for England against New Zealand in 1975, played 267 games for the Black and Whites, scoring 47 tries.

The Eighties and Super League

THE Eighties opened with a return to the Twin Towers of Wembley for the famous all-Humberside Final. The match never lived up to its hype however, and Kingston Rovers defeated Hull in a scrappy game.

Another influx of fresh talent brought Dane O'Hara and James Leuluai from New Zealand and Barry Banks, Tony Dean, Graham Evans and David Topliss. Clive Sullivan and Mick Crane returned to the Boulevard and the average attendance jumped to just below 12,000.

In January 1982 the Airlie Birds defeated their East Hull rivals 12-4 in front of a crowd of 25,165 in the Regal Trophy Final at Headingley.

In February the Black and Whites defeated Salford and Fulham in the Challenge Cup, a victory over Halifax and a semi-final win against Castleford at Headingley put Hull in the Final for the tenth time. At Wembley Widnes and Hull produced the first drawn game since the famous final of 1954 and the reply was set for Elland Road, Leeds 18 days later. In an emotional evening heightened by the glare of the floodlights the Airlie Birds defeated Widnes 14-9 to collect the Challenge Cup for the first time since Bert Gilbert lifted the cup at Thrum Hall in 1914.

Such was the interest in rugby league on Humberside that the club applied to run a second team, Hull White Star, but the visionary venture was turned down by the Rugby Football League.

The Yorkshire Cup was collected for the third time in 1983 and Hull were at Wembley for the third time in four years to oppose Featherstone Rovers. One of the biggest shocks in the history of the competition saw Featherstone beat odds on favourites Hull 14-12 with a late penalty goal.

The Championship was won for the sixth time in the club's history in 1982-83 and Hull were runners up in the Premiership Trophy for the third time.

The 1983-84 season brought another Yorkshire Cup to the Boulevard and the Black and Whites were runners up in the league.

At Wembley in 1985 the Airlie Birds lost to Wigan in one of the finest finals of the modern era. The Yorkshire Cup was collected for the third season in succession and Hull were beaten 12-0 by Kingston Rovers in the Regal Trophy Final at Boothferry Park.

In 1991 Hull collected their last major trophy when they defeated Widnes 14-4 at Old Trafford.

The club slumped a little and in 1995 with the change to summer rugby and the creation of Super League, the Airlie Birds found themselves in the new first division.

In 1997 the club added the name Sharks and gained promotion to Super League as first division champions.

A series of near-disastrous financial crises hit the club and amidst the merger mania of the late 1990s Hull were linked with Hull Kingston Rovers several times.

In 2000 the club merged with Gateshead Thunder, dropped the name Sharks, returned to more traditional black and white shirts and became known simply as Hull FC.

The Rugby Football League
State Express
Challenge Cup
Final
Hull v Hull K.R.
Saturday 3rd. May 1980 Kick-off 3pm
Wembley
Stadium
OFFICIAL PROGRAMME 60p

The cover for the all-Humberside 1980 Challenge Cup Final at Wembley. The Airlie Birds beat Millom and York at the Boulevard, Bradford Northern at Odsal and Widnes at Swinton, in the semi-final, to set up the dream encounter with Kingston Rovers.

Rover's half back Roger Millward and Steve Norton, the two captains, share a word at the final whistle.

The side for the John Player semi-final against Barrow at Headingley on 10 January 1981 are Back row (left to right): Tim Wilby, Barry Banks, Charlie Stone, Paul Woods, Trevor Skerrett, Bob Gaitley and Charlie Birdsall. Front: Graham Bray, Paul Prendiville, Ron Wileman, Steve Norton, Sammy Lloyd and Clive Pickerill. Hull held a slender 3-2 half-time lead but Barrow were victors 13-10.

Paul Prendiville (5), with Steve Norton in support, moves in to tackle Kingston Rovers full-back George Fairbairn during the all-Humberside John Player Trophy Final at Headingley, Leeds.

Widnes prop Brian Lockwood evades the tackle of Ron Wileman during the drawn 1982 Challenge Cup Final at

A jubilant Charlie Stone holds aloft the John Player Trophy following the Black and Whites 12-4 victory over Kingston Rovers at Headingley. Ron Wileman scored a try, Lee Crookes kicked four goals and Tony Dean added a dropped goal.

Lee Crookes, a skillful ball-handling prop and superb goal-kicker, made his debut for Hull on 30 November 1980 and made 196 appearances, scored 44 tries and kicked 389 goals before his transfer to Leeds for a then-record fee of £150,000.

The line-up for the Challenge Cup Final replay at Elland Road, Leeds.

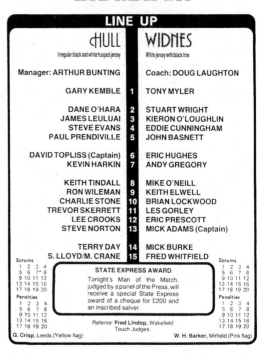

BIG MATCH

LINE UP

cHULL		WIDNES
Irregular black and white hooped jersey		White jersey with black trim
Manager: ARTHUR BUNTING		Coach: DOUG LAUGHTON
GARY KEMBLE	1	TONY MYLER
DANE O'HARA	2	STUART WRIGHT
JAMES LEULUAI	3	KIERON O'LOUGHLIN
STEVE EVANS	4	EDDIE CUNNINGHAM
PAUL PRENDIVILLE	5	JOHN BASNETT
DAVID TOPLISS (Captain)	6	ERIC HUGHES
KEVIN HARKIN	7	ANDY GREGORY
KEITH TINDALL	8	MIKE O'NEILL
RON WILEMAN	9	KEITH ELWELL
CHARLIE STONE	10	BRIAN LOCKWOOD
TREVOR SKERRETT	11	LES GORLEY
LEE CROOKS	12	ERIC PRESCOTT
STEVE NORTON	13	MICK ADAMS (Captain)
TERRY DAY	14	MICK BURKE
S. LLOYD/M. CRANE	15	FRED WHITFIELD

Scrums
1 2 3 4
5 6 7 8
9 10 11 12
13 14 15 16
17 18 19 20
Penalties
1 2 3 4
5 6 7 8
9 10 11 12
13 14 15 16
17 18 19 20

Scrums
1 2 3 4
5 6 7 8
9 10 11 12
13 14 15 16
17 18 19 20
Penalties
1 2 3 4
5 6 7 8
9 10 11 12
13 14 15 16
17 18 19 20

STATE EXPRESS AWARD
Tonight's Man of the Match, judged by a panel of the Press, will receive a special State Express award of a cheque for £200 and an inscribed salver.

Referee: Fred Lindop, Wakefield
Touch Judges:
G. Crisp, Leeds (Yellow flag)   W. H. Barker, Mirfield (Pink flag)

The jubilation and relief shows on the faces of the Hull players with the Challenge Cup at Elland Road. It was the Airlie Birds second Challenge Cup Final victory after a gap of 68 years.

Man of the match David Topliss is hoisted aloft with the Challenge Cup at Elland Road. Topliss crossed for two tries, Lee Crookes and Dane O'Hara each scored one and Lee Crookes kicked four goals.

In 1983 Hull won the race to capture BARLA star Garry Schofield, a skillful centre with a tremendous ability to score tries. He crossed for 37 tries and kicked 57 goals in his first season of professional rugby league and scored a total of 824 points before he was transferred to Leeds in October 1987.

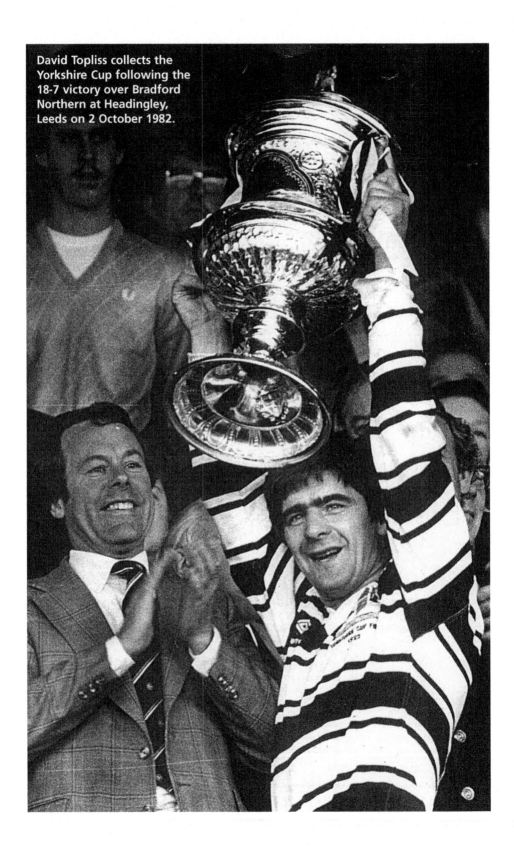

David Topliss collects the Yorkshire Cup following the 18-7 victory over Bradford Northern at Headingley, Leeds on 2 October 1982.

Gary Divorty a strong running loose forward signed from Heworth ARLFC in 1983 and won two Great Britain caps before his £120,000 transfer to Leeds in September 1989.

The 1983 squad at the Boulevard. Back row (left to right): Trevor Skerrett, Terry Day, Phil Edmonds, Lee Crookes, Tim Wilby, Steve Norton. Middle row (players only): Paul Rose, Dane O'Hara, Barry Banks, Keith Bridges, Steve Evans, Gary Kemble, Wayne Proctor and Mick Crane. Seated: Tony Duke, Tony Dean, Kevin Harkin, Dave Topliss, Charlie Stone, Paul Prendiville and James Leuluai.

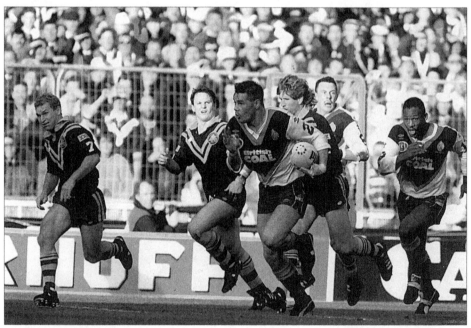

Goal-kicking wingman Paul Eastwood joined Hull from Hullensians Rugby Union club in 1985 and made a total of 13 appearances for Great Britain whilst at the Boulevard.

Peter Sterling the influential Australian half-back joined the Black and Whites from Sydney premiership club Parramatta in 1983-84 making his debut against Wakefield Trinity at Belle Vue, the same day his Kangaroo team mate Wally Lewis made his debut for Trinity.

Lee Jackson, one of the modern game's finest hookers. Jackson made his Hull debut on 16 April 1986 and spent time playing in Australia before re-joining the Airlie Birds from Leeds.

Australian international prop Noel 'Crusher' Cleal joined Hull from Manly in August 1989 and scored nine tries in 25 appearances in his first season at the Boulevard. He took over the coaching duties for a spell when Brian Smith departed.

Paul Harrison, the brother of prop Karl, signed from Featherstone Miners Welfare ARL in September 1988.

Great Britain prop Karl Harrison signed from Featherstone Rovers in August 1989 and was one of the clubs finest forwards of the modern era. He was transferred to Halifax in August 1991 and returned to the Boulevard in December 1998.

Steve McNamara joined Hull from local amateur side Skirlaugh in June 1989 and gained international honours with Great Britain before his move to Bradford Bulls.

Dane O'Hara
pictured here in
March 1989 was one
of the famous trio
of Kiwis signed in
1981.

The Hull front three of Andy Dannatt, Mike Dixon and Karl Harrison prepare to pack down in the first league match of the 1990-91 season against St Helens at the Boulevard. The Airlie Birds defeated Saints 20-14 and ended the season in third place with 17 victories from 26 games.

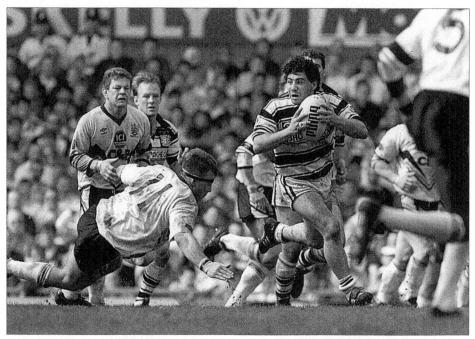

Patrick Entant evades a desperate challenge from Widnes second row Paul Hulme during the 1991 Premiership Final at Old Trafford. Entant, a French international, had signed from Avignon in July 1990.

Hull celebrate the 14-4 Premiership Final triumph over Widnes, the first and only time the Airlie Birds lifted the title.

In 1991 the Kumuls of Papua New Guinea made their second tour of Europe and met a Humberside 13 at the Boulevard on 3 November. Hull's Jon Sharpe, the Humberside captain exchanges pennants with Stanley Haru the Kumuls captain before the game which Humberside won 16-14.

Ian Marlow the Hull prop takes the ball forward during the 1992 Charity Shield match against Wigan at Gateshead.

Wearing their far from traditional away shirts the Hull players line up following another Castleford try during the 34-6 defeat at Wheldon Road in September 1992. The 1992-93 season was a poor one with just ten wins from 26 matches.

The all-action Stanley Gene, a modern era impact player in full flow against London Broncos.

Australian Matt Daylight in full flow against Wigan at the Boulevard.

Steve Craven a
1994-95 signing
from Ryedale York.

Paul Cooke
in action
against
Leeds in the
2001
Challenge
Cup game at
the
Boulevard.

Deon Bird.

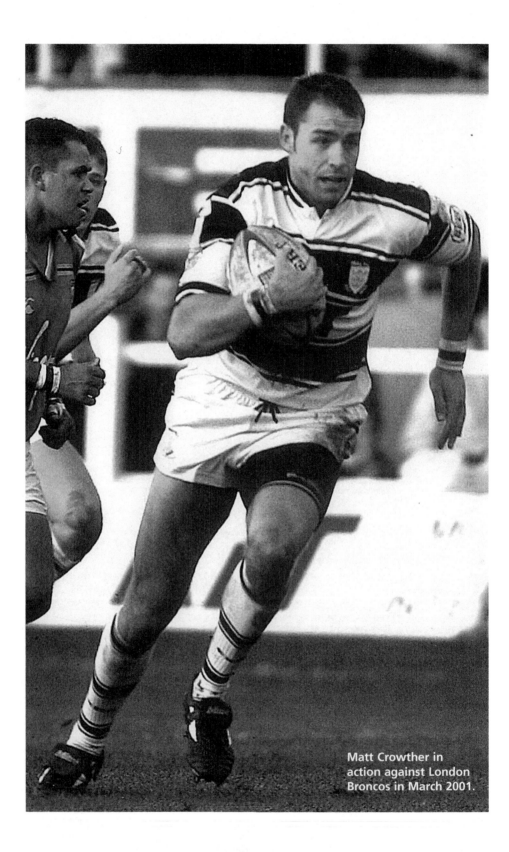

Matt Crowther in action against London Broncos in March 2001.

Will Robinson.

Hull-born Richard Horne, who signed from West Hull ARLFC, one of the young stars of the 2001 season.

Club Records

Records

Highest score: 86-0 v Elland, 1 April 1899

Highest Attendance: 28,798 v Leeds, Challenge Cup, 7 May 1936

Appearances

501 by Edward 'Ned' Rogers 1906 to 1925

Tries

Career: 250 by Clive Sullivan 1961-74 and 1981-85

Season: 52 by Jack Harrison 1914-15

Match: 7 by Clive Sullivan v Doncaster, 5 April 1968

Goals

Career: 687 by Joe Oliver 1928-37 and 1943-45

Season: 170 by Geoff 'Sammy' Lloyd 1978-79

Match: 14 by Geoff 'Sammy' Lloyd v Oldham, 10 September 1978

14 by Jim Kennedy v Rochdale Hornets, 7 April 1921

Points

Career: 1,842 by Joe Oliver 1928-37 and 1943-45

Season: 369 by Geoff 'Sammy' Lloyd 1978-79

Match: 36 by Jim Kennedy v Keighley, 29 January 1921

A cigarette card depicting record points holder Joe Oliver.

Clive Sullivan who scored 250 tries in his career with Hull FC.

Printed in Great Britain
by Amazon

83555226R00099